The Crow
Tarbescu, Edith   Test#: 46803
Points: 1.0   Lvl: 6.6

The Crow

Edith Tarbescu

Franklin Watts
A Division of Grolier Publishing
New York • London • Hong Kong • Sydney
Danbury, Connecticut

Dedicated to the Crow Nation, particularly Burton D. Pretty On Top, Sr., Dale Old Horn, Joseph Medicine Crow, Lawrence and Jennifer Flat Lip; as well as Kevin Kooistra-Manning, Western Heritage Center, Billings, MT; Richard Pittsley, Chief Plenty Coups Museum State Park, Pryor, Montana; and Susan Aller and Pegi Deitz Shea for their friendship and editorial help.

Note to readers: Definitions for words in **bold** can be found in the Glossary at the back of this book.

Photographs ©: American Museum of Natural History: 16; Corbis-Bettmann: 15 (UPI), 26, 28; Courtesy Little Bighorn Battlefield National Monument: 4, 34; Cumberland County Historical Society, Carlisle, PA.: 37, 38; Dembinsky Photo Assoc.: 12 (Jim Battles); Edith Tarbescu: 6, 7; Friends of Chief Plenty Coups Museum: 19, 40; Hardin Photo Service: 36 (Dennis Sanders), 3 top, 44 (Geri Sanders); Larry Mayer: 22, 42, 45; Liaison Agency, Inc.: 20 (Kip Brundage), 11, 46, 47 (Paul Vandevelder); Marilyn "Angel" Wynn: 8; North Wind Picture Archives: 14, 32, 33, 35; Reinhard Brucker: 3 bottom, 17, 18, 24, 25, 27; Smithsonian Institution, Washington, DC: 39 (Anthropological Archives/Photograph by Charles M. Bell. Washington, D.C., 1880); Superstock, Inc.: 29; Tony Stone Images: 49 (Tom Bean); Travel Montana: 48 (Donnie Sexton); Union Pacific Railroad Museum Collection: 31.

Cover illustration by Gary Overacre, interpreted from a photograph (Smithsonian Institution, Washington, DC: (Anthropological Archives/Photograph by Charles M. Bell. Washington, D.C., 1880)

Map by XNR Productions Inc.

Visit Franklin Watts on the Internet at:
http://publishing.grolier.com

Library of Congress Cataloging-in-Publication Data

Tarbescu, Edith.
    The Crow / by Edith Tarbescu.
        p.   cm.— (Watts Library)
    Includes bibliographical references and index.
    ISBN: 0-531-20356-5 (lib. bdg.)   0-531-16470-5 (pbk.)
    1. Crow Indians—History—Juvenile literature. 2. Crow Indians—Social life and customs—Juvenile literature. [1. Crow Indians. 2. Indians of North America—Great Plains.] I. Title. II. Series.
E99.C92T37 2000
973'.04975—DC21   97-47705
                                                                                                                  CIP
                                                                                                                  AC

Contents

When planning for battle, Custer relied on Indian scouts.

Battle of the Little Bighorn

In June 1876, near an Indian village on the Little Bighorn River in Montana, General George Armstrong Custer of the United States Army led his men into the most famous battle between the U.S. Army and the American Indians. They fought the battle—also known as "Custer's Last Stand"—on land that was sacred to the Crow Indians.

Hoping to keep their tribal land by helping the U.S. Army, five members of the Crow **scouted** for General Custer against Sioux, Cheyenne, and Arapaho **warriors**. What events had led to this dramatic moment in American history?

As white men moved westward—years before the Battle of the Little Bighorn—they made permanent changes in the lifestyle and land of the American Indians. These changes

Tourists from all over the world visit the famous battlefield.

included diseases that caused the deaths of thousands of Plains Indians, including the Crow.

By 1876, the Plains resembled a giant checkerboard. As one tribe advanced, another retreated. The Crow were attacked from all sides by people who wanted their land. In addition, herds of buffalo—their main food supply—were being destroyed by white hunters.

The Crow had to make a choice. They could fight against the white man—and possibly lose more land—or they could compromise. They chose to compromise. By scouting for the U.S. Army, as other Indian tribes did, the Crow hoped to keep as much of their land as possible. Some Crow remained neutral, and some supported the Army, but they all had the same goal in mind—to keep their land.

This is the story of the Crow people. It's a story of battles and broken treaties, of **prophecies**, and visions. Most of all, it's the story of a nation and its fight for survival, and how the people of that nation won that battle.

Cave paintings tell the story of an ancient people.

Chapter One

Early History

We know that American Indians lived in North and South America before explorers arrived. But where did they come from?

Some people believe that the Native Americans crossed a land bridge from Asia to North America thousands of years ago. They believe a land bridge across the Bering Strait connected the continents. They say the bridge disappeared when glaciers melted and covered the land with water. The Native Americans then followed the animals they hunted, and settled in the Americas. Some native **bands** traveled as far south as Central and South America.

Crow Territory

The four bands of the Crow lived in the part of North America known as the Great Plains.

However, scholars cannot prove that the Bering land bridge existed. Some believe that the American Indians have always lived in North America.

Originally, there were two Crow bands. The Mountain Crow lived in the southern part of the area that is now Montana and Wyoming, and the River Crow lived north of the Yellowstone River.

Eventually, the Mountain Crow split into a third band of the Crow tribe called Kicked in the Bellies. They got this name when a member of the band saw a horse for the first time. As he bent over to look closely at the animal, the horse reared up and kicked him in the belly. This band was used by a Crow Chief for defense purposes. Eventually, the three groups united. A fourth band, known as the Beaver Which Dries Its Fur, no longer exists.

Today, most of the Crow live in southeastern Montana where their people have lived for hundreds of years. Ancient fossils and oral Crow history suggest that the Mountain Crow may have lived in Montana for more than 11,000 years.

According to history, the Crow were originally hunter-**gatherers** who lived in the Great Lakes region. They were part of another plains group called the Hidatsa. Later, they became farmers, planting corn and squash and living in earthen lodges along the Missouri River. The river became a main source of survival for the Crow. But as the Crow moved away from the river to become hunters, they developed a different lifestyle. They followed the herds of bighorn sheep,

Tepees made a suitable home for a people on the move.

deer, elk, and buffalo that roamed the Plains. They also began living in **tepees**, which were easy to move from place to place.

Buffalo were once plentiful throughout the Plains.

Chapter Two

Lifestyle

After the Crow settled on the Plains, hunting buffalo became the focus of their lives. They ate the meat of the buffalo and used its skin to make tepees and clothing. The women used buffalo **sinew** (tendons connecting muscle to bone) to make sewing thread. The men used buffalo bones for making needles and tools. Before each hunt, the warriors said a prayer thanking the buffalo for giving up its life for the tribe.

Hunting

Before the Crow had guns, they hunted with bows and arrows and spears. By the

The Crow warrior's skill with horses was important in the buffalo hunt.

l600s, the Spanish had brought horses to America, and tribes in the Southwest **bred** wild ponies. As a result of trading between tribes, horses began moving north onto the Plains. Riding on horseback, the Crow were able to expand their hunting grounds and follow the vast herds of buffalo.

Even before they had horses, however, the Crow were inventive and creative. It was hard to hunt buffalo on foot so they would sometimes stampede buffalo herds. The Crow chased the buffalo herd until the animals crashed headlong over cliffs. The Crow name for the so-called buffalo jump is "Driving Buffalo over Embankments."

The buffalo meat was then cut up and carried back to the camps. There the men built fires and cooked the meat over blazing coals. Most of the hunting was done in fall and spring. Fall was a great time for hunting because the animals had **gorged** themselves during the summer to store fat for the cold, winter months.

Food

A good buffalo hunt meant plenty of food for everybody. As the coals heated, people gathered around the fire in preparation for the feast. But the hunters also knew there would be

times when the snow would be so deep that they would be unable to travel in search of buffalo. Then they would be confined to the camp.

To prepare for the long winter, the women dried and smoked the leftover meat. This was called jerky—similar to today's beef jerky.

While fathers taught boys **archery** and hunting, mothers taught girls the skills they would need. During the summer months, women and girls gathered root plants, berries, wild plums, and many other wild plants that they used for food and medicine.

Crow women tanning buffalo hide and drying meat

Buffalo Beware!

Today, buffalo still are hunted for their meat, hide, and horns.

Clothing and Shelter

During winter in the Plains, the cold winds howled through the tall grasses and the cottonwood trees. To keep warm, the Crow used buffalo **hide**. They first **tanned** the hide to make tepees, and then set the tepees up out of the wind. The hide was also used to make warm blankets and robes, and floor coverings for tepees. During the winter, the Crow women used the hide to make coats for themselves and the men in their tribe. The fur of the buffalo was worn on the inside for extra warmth and softness against their skin.

During the hot summer months, Crow men generally wore only **breechcloths** and **moccasins**. But even when it was very hot, women wore long dresses made of deer, elk, or antelope skin. For dancing or ceremonies, they decorated dresses with

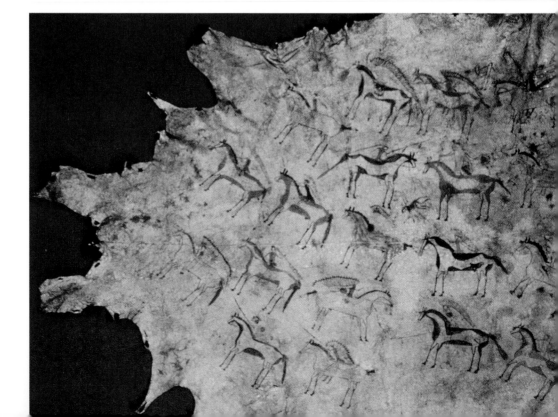

A decorated buffalo hide tells of a Crow battle or hunt.

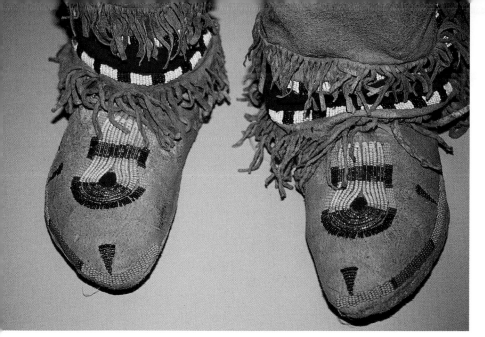

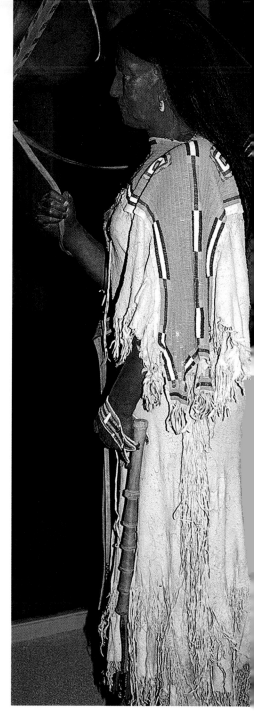

feathers, seeds, seashells, and dyed porcupine **quills**. Soft deer hide was used for these fancy dresses.

In the early 1880s, when the Crow began trading with Europeans for glass beads, women used these beads to decorate nearly everything they owned: dresses, leggings, moccasins, even saddles and horse bridles. To this day, the Crow are known for their beautiful beadwork.

Travel

During the years of hunting buffalo, the Crow were considered **nomads**. The people roamed freely according to the seasons and their food supply.

The Crow women were responsible for taking down and setting up the tepees. With the help of dogs, the band moved frequently from one place to another.

Deer hide moccasins (upper left) and beaded dress (above) in a museum display

This museum exhibit shows how the travois was a useful device.

First the women assembled platforms with long wooden poles on either side of them. The dogs were then harnessed to the poles, so they could pull the platforms behind them. The platform, or **travois** (trah-voy) helped the band carry all their belongings. Years later, the Crow used horses instead of dogs to pull these platforms. Then old people and children were carried on the platforms during long journeys.

Wherever the Crow settled, children played games and swam in clear, running water. There were times when everybody had to help with the chores, but there was also opportunity for fun.

Arts and Storytelling

Until the late 1960s, the Crow had no written language. Their history was passed down from one **generation** to another through storytelling. **Elders** often chose children—sometimes as young as four or five—to be the keepers of these stories. The children were encouraged to listen carefully and remember what they heard.

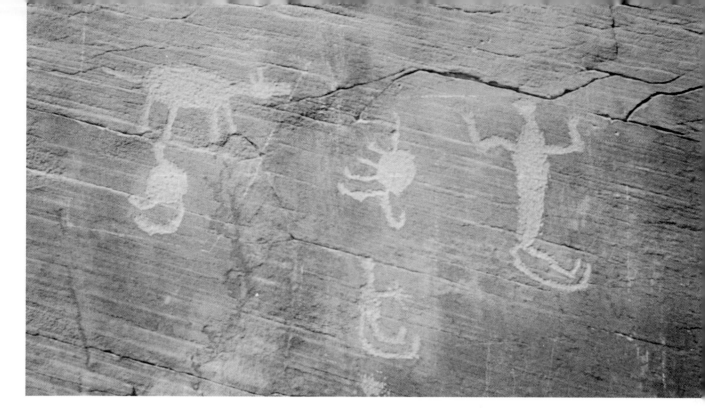

The Crow also kept records of important events, such as buffalo hunts and battles, by making stone etchings in caves. These **etchings** of figures and animals have faded over the centuries, but they still exist. They also kept records by painting on animal skins, such as elk hides.

During the 1800s, the tradition of hide-painting ended. The Plains Indians began drawing in bound ledger books acquired from traders and white soldiers. Using pens, pencils, and watercolors, they drew pictures of hunters, warriors, and dancers.

Many of these drawings were later collected by soldiers as **souvenirs**, then gathered and sold to historians and tourists. Several hundred are in a collection at the Smithsonian's National Museum of the American Indian.

Etchings on wood and stone, though faded, keep the stories of Crow ancestors alive.

Chapter Three

Beliefs

According to Crow legend, the creation of man and woman came from a god named First Maker, who came down to earth one day and looked out across the water. It was at a time when there was hardly any land. The Creator couldn't see anything. Three ducks swam by, so he called them over. He asked one of the ducks to dive down and see what was under the water. The first duck didn't come up with anything, so the Creator sent another duck down.

The second duck came up with a lump of mud that contained clay. "I think I can do something with this," said the

Creator. He reached down and grabbed some clay. He rolled it around in his hands and shaped it into a figure. Then the Creator breathed life into what became the first human beings. He created male and female at the same time.

Later, First Maker said to the man, "Only kill for food, not for fun, and don't kill too many animals." He also said, "Pick berries and catch fish. This is all yours; it's a gift. But remember, don't hurt the animals and don't waste what I have given you."

A Vision Quest

The Pryor Mountains, also known as the Shot Rocks, stand in the midst of the Crow country. On top of the mountains are three large rocks called Castle Rocks or Sacred Rocks. These rocks are very special to the Crow. The Crow travel to the Pryor Mountains on a religious journey called a **vision quest**. Not everyone chooses to go on a vision quest, but those who do feel proud to accomplish it.

Imagine climbing to the top of a steep mountain alone, or with one other person, and staying there without food or drink for four days and four nights. You would endure the heat, cold, or rain, hoping for a vision or dream. During this time, you would pray to First Maker, asking him to help your people.

During the days of **warfare**, a person on a vision quest hoped to see an animal or an eagle appear in a vision. Then that person would carry or wear eagle feathers or fur from that animal. These articles were considered to have magical

The Pryor Mountains

The Little People

Another traditional Crow belief concerns the Little People. In a gap between the rocks on Pryor Mountain, the Crow believe there is a lodge where the Little People live.

They believe that the Little People are ghost-like beings, much like humans but only about 2 to 3.5 feet (60 to 90 cm) tall. A few Crow claim to have seen the Little People, but many who have never seen the Little People still believe in them. They believe that they are either spirits, half-spirit and half-flesh, or all flesh.

In the past, many Plains Indians were afraid of the Little People and their powers. But the Crow always believed that the Little People protected them from enemies.

powers, like lucky charms. The Europeans eventually called those magical powers "medicine," but the American Indians never used this term. The expression "Indian medicine" came from the white man, as did as **"papoose," "squaw," "tomahawk," "tom-tom,"** and many others.

Many members of the Crow Nation still carry on the tradition of a vision quest. Although most people are weak from hunger and thirst afterward, they gain a sense of purpose, strength, and awe from this life-changing experience.

A Crow rifle case

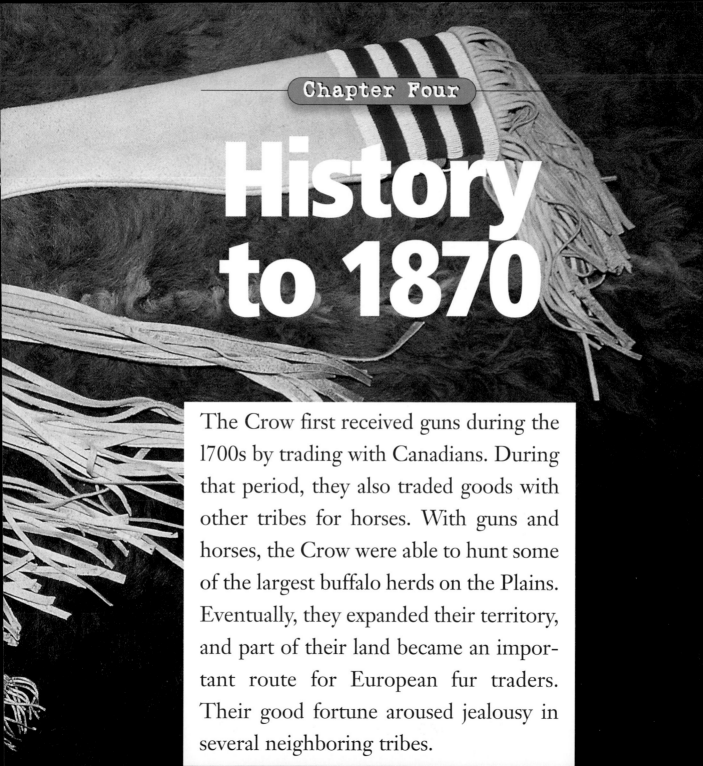

Chapter Four

History to 1870

The Crow first received guns during the 1700s by trading with Canadians. During that period, they also traded goods with other tribes for horses. With guns and horses, the Crow were able to hunt some of the largest buffalo herds on the Plains. Eventually, they expanded their territory, and part of their land became an important route for European fur traders. Their good fortune aroused jealousy in several neighboring tribes.

Tribes of the Northern Plains fought each other for land and horses.

As a result, Crow warriors often had to fight to protect their land. They fought against Shoshone raiders from the south, Blackfeet enemies from the north, Flathead from the west, and Sioux hunters from the east.

The Sioux Indians, the largest tribe on the Plains at that time, acquired most of their territory from other tribes. Before the Europeans began forcing the Sioux from their sacred Black Hills (*Xe Sapa*), the Sioux attacked the Crow because they wanted their land, too. Sometimes, the Crow led **raiding** parties to capture horses from neighboring tribes. But the Crow generally fought to defend their honor—and later, their land.

After the White Men

Before Europeans moved into the West, the Crow rarely saw a white man. Lewis and Clark had a brief encounter with the Crow in 1805 and 1806 when the two men were sent by President Thomas Jefferson to explore the region. Traveling westward from the Missouri River, Lewis and Clark were looking for a route to the Pacific Ocean.

At this time, **trading posts** were being built. When fur traders began traveling west, the Crow exchanged their furs for various European items, including the glass beads they used to decorate their clothing. In addition, the Crow escorted European fur traders across American Indian territory as far west as Idaho and Washington.

A trading post as it may have looked during the time of Lewis and Clark.

The Name "Crow"

The Europeans called them the Crow Indians. But their real name is *Apsaalooke* (pronounced ab-sah-lo-ga). French explorers thought this word meant "large bird" which they interpreted as "raven" or "crow."

According to Crow oral history, *Apsaalooke* means "something sharp and pointed," like a weapon. The LeVerendrye brothers, who worked for the Hudson's Bay Company of Canada, probably misnamed the Crow. However, the name "Children of the Large-Beaked Bird" is the popular meaning, and many Crow refer to themselves that way.

"Old Hickory" Andrew Jackson (1767-1845) was the seventh U.S. president.

The U.S. Government and New Settlers

The Crow leaders signed several treaties with the U. S. government, hoping their people could live in peace. But this was not to happen.

Chief Long Hair of the Mountain Crow signed their first **treaty**, the Friendship Treaty, with the United States in 1825. But in 1830, President Andrew Jackson's Indian Removal Act began forcing Indians west, making life hard for all Native Americans.

In 1851, the Fort Laramie Treaty established boundaries for the "Indian Country." This was land for several Plains tribes, including the Crow. But another Fort Laramie treaty in 1868 greatly reduced the Crow territory.

By the mid-1800s, white settlers were traveling in covered wagons bound for Oregon and California. Many had heard that there was plenty of land out west. The treaties between the American Indians and the U.S. government became mean-

Indian Removal Act

The Indian Removal Act, signed in 1830, gave the president power to negotiate removal treaties with Indian tribes living east of the Mississippi. Under these treaties, the Indians were to give up their lands east of the Mississippi in exchange for lands to the west. Those who wished to remain in the east would become citizens of their home state. The removal was supposed to be voluntary and peaceful, but Jackson forced the resisting southeastern nations to leave. Thousands of Indians died in the forced migration.

ingless, and more of their land was taken away. Before long, herds of cattle and fences appeared all over Crow territory.

Hoping for peace, the Crow signed a treaty in 1868 with the United States, giving up 30 million acres (12 million hectares) of land. But that treaty turned out to be one of the most treacherous and devastating events in Crow history. It eventually led to the opening of the route for the Union Pacific Railroad. The building of the railroad marked the end for the Plains buffalo— the Crow's source of food and shelter.

Eventually, European traders brought the Crow something that changed their lives forever—diseases such as smallpox, measles, and **tuberculosis**. Tepees were filled with sick and dying people, suffering from "white scabs," or smallpox. The disease spread rapidly, hitting children especially hard.

Since traders carried these diseases, many white people also died. But the American Indians had never been exposed to

Settlers moved across the Plains— into the heart of Crow territory— in search of farmland and a new prosperity.

29

these infections and they were devastating. Their immune systems had no defenses against smallpox—or even less severe diseases such as measles. Although many American Indian tribes had been given **vaccines** against smallpox, the Crow were never vaccinated.

The Crow were nearly wiped out by smallpox. Between 1843 and 1845, the Crow population dropped from about 8,000 to fewer than 2,000. The Crow population has since grown to approximately 10,000.

Not only was their population greatly reduced by European diseases during this period, but the Crow had to learn to live with European people and customs. They had to accept the fact that land, which they called Mother Earth, could be bought and sold.

Killing off the Buffalo

After the Crow sold that huge amount of land to the United States in 1868, the tribe still faced problems. Gold was discovered on the Yellowstone River, and hundreds of **prospectors** began entering the Crow's western lands.

Before long, the government granted millions of acres of land *free* to the railroads. Then the rail companies took out newspaper advertisements selling land along the tracks. People rushed westward, and before long, dozens of towns were built.

The railroad companies wanted to expand their business and encourage European settlers to move into the Plains. They couldn't remove the American Indians from their land,

A Great Loss

There had once been approximately 50 million buffalo on the North American continent. By 1888, fewer than 500 animals remained.

so they decided to get rid of their main food supply—the buffalo. Hunters from the East were encouraged—and even paid—to shoot buffalo from open windows on the trains passing through the Plains. Unlike the American Indians, the Europeans used only a small part of the buffalo and left the rest to rot. General Philip Sheridan said, "Let the buffalo hunters kill, skin, and sell until the buffalo is exterminated, as it is the only way to bring lasting peace and allow civilization to advance."

Homesteaders moved in, and cattle or "spotted buffalo" replaced the buffalo herds. In 1870, the U.S. government confined the Crow to a **reservation**. They could no longer move about freely. Then an event occurred that changed the fate of the Crow, and all Native Americans, forever.

Killing buffalo for sport from the comfort of a railroad car

A view of the Little Bighorn River, near the battlefield

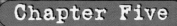
History from 1870

The sun scorched the earth on June 25, 1876. It was a day that would forever change the fate of the Crow, and all other Native Americans. Perched high on a hill, in a hideout called the Crow's Nest, a seventeen-year-old Crow scout named Curley looked down on a tribal village. He was one of five Crow and forty Arikara Indian scouts hired by General George Armstrong Custer.

Before the battle, the Arikara scouts spotted an enormous herd of horses, as

Curley was one of the few surviving eye-witnesses of the Battle of the Little Bighorn.

well as thousands of tepees in the distance. The scouts warned Custer that he didn't have a chance battling thousands of Sioux, Cheyenne, and Arapaho warriors. But Custer called the scouts cowards and didn't listen to them.

Most of the scouts rode off, including Curley. As he galloped away, Curley used field glasses to watch the end of Custer and his men. They were surrounded by thousands of warriors. Custer and his entire **regiment** of 210 soldiers never advanced beyond the hill, now called Last Stand Hill. The warriors killed them in a matter of minutes. A Sioux warrior who was there said, "The Indians charged toward Custer's troops like a hurricane. . . . like bees let out of a hive."

Custer's arrogance led to his defeat. "I could whip all the Indians on the continent with the Seventh Cavalry," he had boasted. Custer (the "boy-general," who had been made a general at the age of twenty-three during the Civil War) was known throughout the West as a fierce Indian fighter. He was so eager to taste victory that day that he acted recklessly. He made a great mistake by dividing his troops against an enemy that greatly outnumbered his forces and by not listening to his scouts.

Ironically, Custer immediately became a national hero. Since 1876, dozens of books and movies have told how brave Custer was. Until 1991, the place of battle was called Custer Battlefield National Monument. But many people had complained that it was the only battlefield named for a losing gen-

Simple grave markers on the battlefield today

eral so Congress voted to rename the battlefield the Little Bighorn National Monument.

While Custer's legend grew, Curley—the Crow scout—was called a liar even though he had been working for the U.S. Army. It wasn't until many years later, when Curley was an old man, that people realized that he had told the truth. Many people refused to believe Curley because they couldn't accept that Custer had used such poor judgment. Although no one will know exactly what happened on Last Stand Hill, many people, including historians, now recognize that Curley was telling the truth.

After the Battle

After Custer lost the Battle of the Little Bighorn, U.S. troops came back and burned the warriors' village. Later, the Sioux, Cheyenne, and Arapaho were additionally punished. All three tribes lost enormous amounts of land. The Crow, who had allied themselves with the U.S. military, lost millions of acres of land. But although the federal government now owns most of the Little Bighorn Battlefield, it is surrounded by Crow territory.

In 1870, when the Crow began living on a reservation, they were expected to adapt to the white man's way of life. Some people tried farming, but the Crow had forgotten the skills they once had. The land was dry because it didn't rain often.

Reservation life also meant that the Crow were increasingly dependent on the federal government for food, blankets, and medical supplies. The Crow even had to carry a ticket whenever they traveled on or off the reservation. The survival of the tribe was fragile—and harder times awaited.

Women on the reservation continued their ancient skills.

Taking the Children

Imagine being taken from your home, your family, and your friends. That is what happened to many of the children of the Plains Indians, including the Crow.

To the Crow, children are treasures. They believe it takes an entire village to raise one child. But there was a time, starting in the late 1800s, when Crow children were taken from their families and placed in boarding schools. Some families ran into the hills to hide their children. The boarding-school project became so enormous that the government eventually turned the matter over to religious **missionaries**.

Indian schoolchildren were expected to adopt the culture of the white man.

The people who ran the schools wanted the children to eat better and dress better than they did on the reservation. They wanted to teach the children to live in the white man's world. Once the children arrived at school, they were forbidden to speak their native language and were physically punished if they disobeyed. They were not allowed to wear traditional clothing, or go home for weekends or holidays. Their long hair was cut short, and they had to wear drab uniforms.

At the Carlisle School, a federal boarding school in Pennsylvania, children from about forty different tribes were separated so that they would forget the life and language they left behind. Crow children were not allowed to speak their native

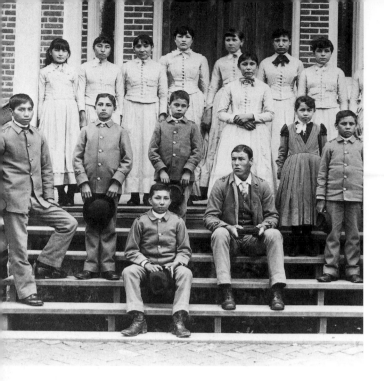

These Crow children entered the Carlisle School around 1890.

language and children of the same tribe were not allowed to share a room.

When Crow children returned to the reservation, many felt they did not belong anywhere—neither in the white man's world nor among their own people. They couldn't remember the Crow language. They weren't raised hearing Crow stories and legends. But because the stories of the Crow oral tradition are so strong, most have survived.

Chief Plenty Coups

It is hard to imagine how much land once belonged to the Crow. In many towns today, a house sits on a 1/2 acre (0.2 ha) of land. In the West, the Crow were forced to give up 65 million acres (26 million ha) of land. The Crow people who had once roamed the prairies hunting buffalo herds now had to adjust to life on the reservation without buffalo for food, and their people nearly starving.

Plenty Coups, the last great chief, came to the Crow when they needed a strong leader. He became chief of the Crow Nation in 1904 and helped guide his people through great change. Many Crow members didn't approve of Chief Plenty Coups, because he had signed away a part of their land in a treaty. But in many ways, he is a hero.

When he was a young boy, Plenty Coups' father died. He was encouraged by his mother and uncles to be fearless. As a child, he had visions that he would be a leader of his people. To prepare himself, he swam in icy cold waters. He also rubbed butterfly wings on his chest, hoping to gain the grace and endurance of a butterfly.

Chief Plenty Coups became known by the U.S. government as the "Chief of Chiefs" in 1921, after the burial ceremony of America's unknown soldier. There, he represented all Indian tribes. Following the ceremony, Chief Plenty Coups placed his warbonnet on the Tomb of the Unknown Soldier.

Like Chief Long Hair before him, Plenty Coups believed that survival for his people meant adjusting to the white man living on their home-

Chief Plenty Coups

lands. He boasted that he never fought against the white man, and was proud of being a scout for the U. S. Army during the 1870s.

Plenty Coups made several trips to Washington, D.C. During one trip, he visited Mount Vernon, the home of George Washington. As an old man, he spoke about Washington's home and how it had inspired him. He said, "I sent my thoughts to the Great White Chief in that other life. I spoke to him, and I believe he heard me. I said, 'Great Chief, as you helped your people, help me now, a Crow chief, to lead

President Warren G. Harding (center) and Chief Plenty Coups (second from left) at the 1921 burial ceremonies in Washington D.C.

my people to peace. I, too, have a little country to save for my children.'"

In 1928, Chief Plenty Coups gave approximately 188 acres (76 ha), including his log house, to Bighorn County to serve as a place where American Indians and other Americans could learn to respect each other's cultures.

In addition to being a traditional chief, Plenty Coups led his people to peace. Since his death in 1932, many Crow refer to him as "the last great chief."

Today, a tribal council with elected officials runs the Crow nation, rather than one chief. Anyone who is at least one-quarter Crow and over the age of eighteen can vote in the election.

Plenty Coups means "many war achievements." And today his famous words still echo across the reservation just as he spoke them to his people. "With education, you are the white man's equal, without it, you are his victim."

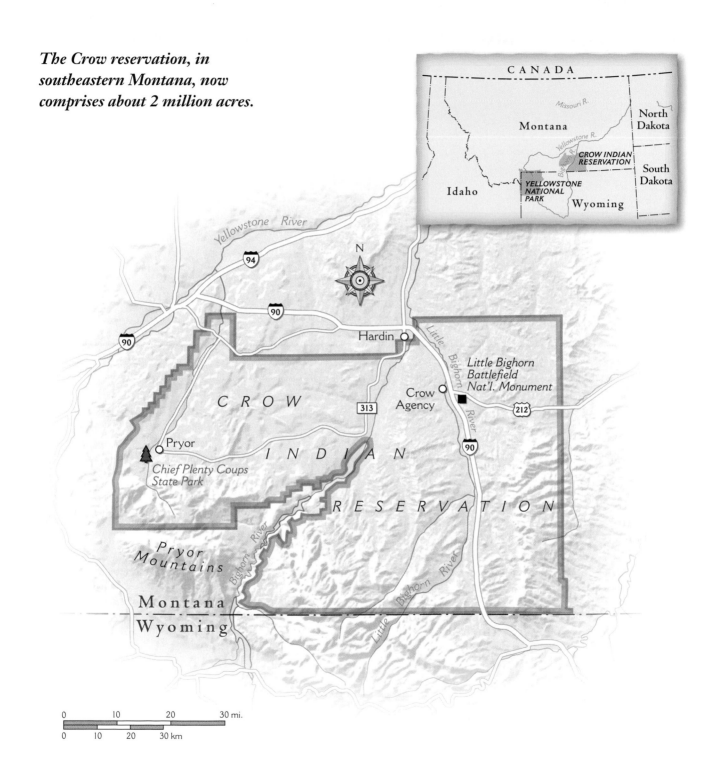

The Crow reservation, in southeastern Montana, now comprises about 2 million acres.

CANADA

Montana

North Dakota

South Dakota

Idaho

Wyoming

YELLOWSTONE NATIONAL PARK

CROW INDIAN RESERVATION

Missouri R.

Yellowstone R.

Big Horn R.

Yellowstone River

94

90

N

90

Hardin

Little Bighorn River

Crow Agency

313

Little Bighorn Battlefield Nat'l. Monument

212

90

C R O W

I N D I A N

R E S E R V A T I O N

Pryor

Chief Plenty Coups State Park

Pryor Mountains

Bighorn River

Little Bighorn River

Montana

Wyoming

0   10   20   30 mi.

0   10   20   30 km

*Camping out at the
Crow Fair*

Chapter Six

Life on the Reservation Today

Today, several schools on the reservation teach the Crow language and culture. The reservation also boasts a two-year college—Little Bighorn Community College—where Crow Studies and the Crow language are part of the program. The Crow are striving to preserve their heritage and pass their values on to the next generation.

Lots of Tepees

Because so many people set up their tepees on the fairgrounds, the Crow Fair has come to be known as "The Tepee Capital of the World."

Despite their hardships, the Crow consider themselves lucky. Although their land has been greatly reduced, they still occupy approximately 2 million acres (809,374 ha) of land.

The Crow Fair

The Crow Fair, or powwow, is a family reunion, a celebration of the Crow's survival throughout the four seasons. It is a recreation of the gatherings that began hundreds of years ago when band chiefs, village chiefs, and clan chiefs came together for meetings.

This fair, an annual event since 1902, is the result of hard work and love. Women spend months sewing and beading just as their mothers and grandmothers did before them. Beading 1 inch (2.5 cm) of material can take up to one hour.

Thousands of people attend the fair, including many tribal members who travel to Montana from as far away as New Mexico and Arizona. Hundreds of tepees are set up on the fairgrounds.

The day begins as camp criers call on all Crow people to prepare for the parade. While those in the parade get ready, children arrive early, so they can watch the parade up close. The marching begins with veterans of the U.S. Armed Forces carrying flags.

A Crow family assembles the frame of their tepee.

44

Floats follow, carrying men, women and children, all dressed in traditional clothes. Some people choose to march, others ride horseback while others ride horses and ponies decorated with deerskin hides and colorful beads.

After the parade, people enter the **arbor**, which is filled with wooden benches, and await the arrival of the dancers. The grand entry is ablaze with color as dancers enter the circle.

During the competitions, men and women dance separately. The men dance first, wearing beaded moccasins. The dancers keep time to the drums beating out ancient rhythms.

Boys in their regalia wait to march in the grand entry.

A Crow fancy dancer

During the Grass Dance, the fringes on the men's outfits move like the prairie grasses swaying in the wind.

The women come into the ring next. Their dances include the Jingle Dance, the Fancy Shawl, and the Traditional Crow-Style. Using quick, intricate steps, each dancer takes her turn in the circle under the blazing, blue sky. But the dancers never stop, and never give up. They have prepared for this festival all year.

The best dancers—male and female—win money in each category. Some dancers even travel the powwow circuit during the year, in hopes of winning more money.

Other exciting events are going on during the dancing. Rodeos and horse racing are also favorites at the fair. The Crow are famous for their skill with horses.

The Crow Poets

In March 1994, eight student writers from the Crow reservation schools, accompanied by parents and chaperones, visited Washington, D.C. They were the guests of Rita Dove, an African-American Pulitzer Prize winner and U.S. poet laureate. The eight students, also known as the "Crow Poets," were the first members of their tribe, or any other American Indian group, invited to participate in the Library of Congress Poetry and Literature series.

Some rough riding at the Crow Fair rodeo

Dressed in traditional clothing, the students read their poems to a large gathering. The following day, they visited the Tomb of the Unknown Soldier for a wreath-laying ceremony.

Following the ceremony, the students entered a nearby building filled with military **memorabilia**. A glass case in a corner held American Indian items. There students saw the warbonnet, flag, and coup sticks of Chief Plenty Coups. They were his gifts to America following the 1921 dedication of the Tomb of the Unknown Soldier.

Where Are the Crow?

These lines from a poem titled "Where Are the Crow?" written by Charles Yarlott, then an eighth-grader at Pretty Eagle School, reveal how strongly the Crow children feel about their heritage.

*I pick up a book about Indian
    tribes in America.
The Crow appear as one word
In a list of Plains Indians.
In another book about American
    Indians
The Crow have a few pictures.
But even if we are invisible to
    others,
We know who we are,
I know who I am,
I am a Crow.
We have been here a long time,
And I am proud.*

The Crow have survived. Their pride in the Crow language and heritage shows in their annual fair but more importantly, in their everyday lives. Their legends have not been forgotten. Their customs endure, and their children are still their treasures.

If you stand on the plains of Montana and listen closely, the sound of a bird or the wind will whisper in your ear. And the voice will say, "We are the Crow Nation. We're still here. And we intend to remain on our land forever."

The Crow have a sacred bond with the buffalo and with the land.

Timeline of the Crow Nation

1675–1735	Crow tribe and northern Plains Indians acquired horses from Native Americans near Great Salt Lake. (Horses were reintroduced to southwest American Indians by the Spaniards.)
1743	The Apsaalooke (Crow) saw white men for the first time near the present-day town of Hardin, Montana. These were the LeVerendrye brothers from Canada.
1805–1806	Lewis and Clark traveled across Crow country. Clark met the Apsaalooke at Pompey's Pillar.
1824	Bureau of Indian Affairs established.
1825	The Crow sign their first treaty (Friendship Treaty) with the United States.
1830	President Andrew Jackson's Indian Removal Act forces tribes east of the Mississippi to move west.
1832	Funds were appropriated by U.S. Congress for vaccination of some Indian tribes against smallpox. The Crow were not vaccinated.
1843–1845	Epidemic of smallpox reduced Crow population from over 8,000 to fewer than 1,000. (Today, the population is about 10,000.)
1850	First siege of Crow lands by Sioux. The Crow won, keeping their homelands.
1851	Treaty of Fort Laramie with the U.S. government. Crow country reduced to 38 million acres (15 million ha).
1862	The Homestead Act gave 160 acres (65 ha) of Indian land to settlers for $1.25 per acre (0.4 ha).
1864	The Sioux, Cheyenne, and Arapaho tried to annihilate the Crow but failed. The battle took place 7 miles (11 km) north of what is now Pryor, Montana.

1868	Second treaty of Fort Laramie between U.S. government and Native Americans. Crow country reduced to 8 million acres (3.2 million ha), after the United States broke the treaty of 1851.
1871	Extension of transcontinental railways across the West.
1884	Crow Agency moved near Bighorn and Little Bighorn junction by the Bureau of Indian Affairs.
1888	Crow tribe confined to reservation.
1893	Secretary of the Interior Hoke Smith (under President Grover Cleveland's Administration) came to Crow Agency to purchase part of Crow Reservation.
1903	Annual Crow Fair established.
1905	Crow territory reduced to approximately 2 million acres (809,374 ha).
1921	Chief Plenty Coups, the last traditional leader of the Crow Nation, represented all American Indians at the Tomb of the Unknown Soldier at Arlington National Cemetery in Washington, D.C., by placing his warbonnet on the sacred shrine.
1961	Court of Claims awarded $10 million to Crow Nation for land taken from them by federal government since 1851.
1973	Indian voting age lowered to 18 years to conform with the 26th Amendment of the U.S. Constitution.
1973	Office of Indian Rights, formed in Department of Justice 182 years after United States Bill of Rights.
1978	Crow Tribe files coal severance tax suit against Montana.
1987	Supreme Court awards Apsaalooke Indians millions of dollars from state of Montana in Crow coal severance tax case.
1993	Crow Nation begins construction of a new hospital on the Crow reservation for all Crow and Cheyenne people, funded by the United States government.
1990–2000	Madam Chairwoman Clara Nomee heads the Crow Nation's Tribal Council.

Glossary

arbor—a shelter of vines or branches

archery—the practice or skill of shooting with bow and arrow

band—a group of persons acting together for a common purpose

bred—raised animals under controlled conditions

breechcloth—cloth worn around the hips, often as the only covering in warm climates

elder—an older person having authority due to age and experience

etching—drawings produced on a hard surface, such as stone

gatherer—someone who collects food from the wild

generation—all the people of about the same age

gorged—stuffed to capacity

hide—the skin of an animal

homesteader—someone who settles on public land

memorabilia—things that are remarkable and worthy of remembrance

missionaries—people who try to convince others of the truth of a religious belief

moccasin—a soft leather shoe, often made from deer skin

nomads—people who move from place to place, according to weather conditions and food supply

papoose—an American Indian baby

prophecy—a prediction of something to come, often divinely inspired

prospector—someone who explores an area, especially for mineral deposits

quill—a hollow, sharp spine of a porcupine or hedgehog

raid—a surprise attack by a small group of people

regiment—a military unit

reservation—an area of land set apart for a certain use

scout—a person sent out to get information

sinew—a tough cord of connective tissue that joins muscle to bone

souvenir—something that is kept as a reminder of a person or an event

squaw—an American Indian woman

tanned—turned a hide to leather by soaking it in a special liquid

tepee—a small cone-shaped tent, usually made of animal skins

tomahawk—a small ax used by North American Indians

tom-tom—a small drum, usually beaten with the hands

trading post—a station where trading of goods takes place.

travois—a simple vehicle used by Plains Indians, consisting of two poles and a platform

treaty—an agreement in writing between two nations

tuberculosis—a disease that affects the lungs

vaccine—a substance that protects people from a disease

vision quest—a religious journey during which a person has a dream or vision and perhaps meets an animal spirit guide

warfare—war; conflict

warrior—a person engaged in war or struggle

To Find Out More

Books

Bachrach, Deborah. *Custer's Last Stand: Opposing Viewpoints* (Great Mysteries series). San Diego, CA: Greenhaven, 1990.

Doherty, Craig A. and Katherine M. Doherty. *Crow* (Native American Peoples series). Vero Beach, FL: Rourke Publications, 1993.

Greene, Jacqueline D. *Powwow: A Good Day to Dance.* Danbury, CT: Franklin Watts, 1998.

Henckel, Mark. *Battle of Little Bighorn.* Helena, MT: Falcon Publishing, 1992.

Kavasch, E. Barrie. *Crow Children and Elders Talk Together.* New York, Rosen, 1998.

Steedman, Scott. *How Would You Survive as an American Indian?* Danbury, CT: Franklin Watts, 1996.

Videos

Contrary Warriors: A Film of the Crow Tribe. Describes the Crow's battle to preserve their language, family, and culture. (Direct Cinema Ltd. 800-525-0000)

Last Stand at Little Bighorn (The American Experience). Examines the battle, using journals, oral accounts, Indian ledger drawings, archival footage, and feature films. (PBS 800-344-3337)

Native Americans, The Plains. Part I: All Our Relations. Native Americans tell their own story of the tribes that lived on the Great Plains, including the Crow, Sioux, Comanche, and others. (Turner Home Entertainment 800-523-0823)

Organizations and Online Sites

Chief Plenty Coups Museum State Park
Box 100
Pryor, MT 59066
http://www.plentycoups.org/
Take an electronic field trip and explore the life and times of the last great leader of the Crow tribe. Other features include student activities, chat, educator and parents' information, and links to related sites.

Crow Indian Reservation
http://kids.state.mt.us/db__engine/presentations/
presentation.asp?pid=174&sub=Tribal + Histories
These pages are part of the Montana Kids site and will help you learn more about this special part of the state's history and culture.

Custer Battlefield Historical and Museum Association
http://www.cbhma.org/
Learn the history of the Battle of the Little Bighorn, read biographies of Custer, Sitting Bull, and others, and visit the battlefield as it looks today.

Little Bighorn Battlefield National Monument
P.O. Box 39
Crow Agency, MT 59022
http://www.nps.gov/libi/index.htm
This site is maintained by the National Park Service and includes information on lodging, activities, directions to the monument, and more.

A Note on Sources

Several years ago, I met with Burton Pretty On Top, Sr., who was then Public Relations Director for the Crow Nation. He spoke to me about the values and history of the Crow Nation and recommended books to me.

I returned for the annual Crow Fair, held the third weekend in August. At that time, I also visited Chief Plenty Coups Museum State Park in Pryor, Montana, and met with Park Manager Rich Pittsley.

In addition, I met with Lawrence and Jennifer Flat Lip. At Jennifer's invitation, I sat in on a class at St. Charles Catholic School in Pryor, where Jennifer was then teaching elementary school. I also visited the Little Bighorn Community College on the reservation. In addition, I was helped by Dale Old Horn, who agreed to read my manuscript and make comments and suggestions.

During one summer, I visited the Pictograph Caves, located 15 miles (28 km) from Billings, Montana. I also visited the Western Heritage Center in Billings, and spoke at length with Kevin Kooistra-Manning, Community Historian at the center.

After taking a self-guided tour of the Little Bighorn Battlefield, Crow Agency, Montana, I visited the museum. Closer to home, I went to the Smithsonian National Museum of the American Indian in New York City several times. I specifically went one day to hear Joseph Medicine Crow, tribal elder and oral historian, address a group of schoolchildren. He had traveled from Montana to be a guest of the museum.

I watched the Ken Burns series on American Indians, shown on PBS, and I subscribe to *Native Peoples* Magazine.

I also have to thank Crickette Wilke of Dodson, Montana, whom I met for the first time the night before her son's wedding to my daughter in Billings, Montana. When Crickette told me that she was part American Indian and part Jewish, we said we would exchange information. I would help her learn about Judaism, and she would help me understand the culture of American Indians. I don't know how much I taught her, but she inspired me to travel west and learn more about American Indians.

—*Edith Tarbescu*

Index

Numbers in *italics* indicate illustrations.

About the Author

Edith Tarbescu is an author and playwright who studied at the Yale School of Drama. Her children's books include *Annushka's Voyage*, a picture book about Ellis Island, published by Clarion Books. This was chosen as a Notable Children's Trade Book in the Field of Social Studies for 1999. Her other books include *Bring Back My Gerbil*! an Early Reader, published by Scholastic Inc., and *The Boy Who Stuck Out His Tongue* (A Hungarian Folktale), published by Barefoot Books.

Her play *Molly's Boots* won Honorable Mention in the University of Anchorage Native Peoples Drama Contest and had a staged reading at the Edward Albee Theater Conference, in Valdez, Alaska. Her plays have had workshops and productions at various regional theaters around the country, including New York City.

She has relocated to a small town near Santa Fe, New Mexico. There she and her husband Jack enjoy collecting Native American pottery as well as exploring new territories.